CW01663444

A CENTURY *of* NOTTINGHAM

Decorations on South Parade for the Coronation of King George VI and Queen Elizabeth in 1937. Nottingham, like all other cities and towns in the country, dressed their streets and buildings in celebration of the new monarchs.

A CENTURY *of* NOTTINGHAM

DOUGLAS WHITWORTH

SUTTON PUBLISHING

First published in the United Kingdom in 1999 by
Sutton Publishing Limited · Phoenix Mill
Thrupp · Stroud · Gloucestershire · GL5 2BU

Copyright © Douglas Whitworth, 1999
Copyright © 'Britain: A Century of Change', Roger Hudson, 1999

All rights reserved. No part of this publication may be reproduced, stored in a retrieval system, or transmitted, in any form or by any means, electronic, mechanical, photocopying, recording or otherwise, without the prior permission of the publisher and copyright holder.

Douglas Whitworth has asserted the moral right to be identified as the author of this work.

British Library Cataloguing in Publication Data
A catalogue record for this book is available from the British Library.

ISBN 0-7509-2418-7

Front endpaper: Angel Row, *c.* 1910. In the foreground and also behind the statue of Queen Victoria is the pot market, where traders spread out their wares on straw and in baskets for customers to make their choice.
Back endpaper: The city centre viewed from the Newton Building of the Nottingham Trent University in 1996.
Half title page: Drury Hill in 1946. This was a quick way up from Broad Marsh to Middle Pavement, or a street in which to linger while window shopping in a book or antique shop.
Title page: Lister Gate in 1960. This area claimed to have the premier cash trade shops in the city with Woolworths, British Home Stores, C & A Modes and Marks & Spencer the major shops.

To Margaret, with love

ALAN SUTTON™ and SUTTON™ are the
trade marks of Sutton Publishing Limited

Typeset in 11/14pt Photina.
Typesetting and origination by
Sutton Publishing Limited.
Printed in Great Britain by
The Bath Press, Bath.

Contents

Porters with a trolley loaded with cases and parcels are the focal point of this study of the Victoria Railway Station in 1960. Sun pouring through the glass roof transforms an ordinary scene into one of beauty.

Britain: A Century of Change

Children gathered around an early wireless set in the 1920s. The speed and forms of communication were to change dramatically as the century advanced. (*Barnaby's Picture Library*)

The delirious rejoicing at the news of the Relief of Mafeking, during the Boer War in May 1900, is a colourful historical moment. But, in retrospect, the introduction that year of the first motor bus was rather more important, signalling another major adjustment to town life. In the previous 60 years railway stations, post-and-telegraph offices, police and fire stations, gas works and gasometers, new livestock markets and covered markets, schools, churches, football grounds, hospitals and asylums, water pumping stations and sewerage plants had totally altered the urban scene, as the country's population tripled and over 70 per cent were born in or moved to the towns.

When Queen Victoria died in 1901, she was measured for her coffin by her grandson Kaiser Wilhelm, the London prostitutes put on black mourning and the blinds came down in the villas and terraces spreading out from the old town centres. These centres were reachable by train and tram, by the new bicycles and still newer motor cars, connected by the new telephone, and lit by gas or even electricity. The shops may have been full of British-made cotton and woollen clothing but the grocers and butchers were selling cheap Danish bacon, Argentinian beef, Australasian mutton, tinned or dried fish and fruit from Canada, California and South Africa. Most of these goods were carried in British-built-and-crewed ships, burning Welsh steam coal.

Women working as porters on the Great Western Railway, Paddington, *c.* 1917. (*W.L. Kenning/Adrian Vaughan Collection*)

As the first decade moved on, the Open Spaces Act meant more parks, bowling greens and cricket pitches. The first state pensions came in, together with higher taxation and death duties. These were raised mostly to pay for the new Dreadnought battleships needed to maintain naval superiority over Germany, and deter them from war. But the deterrent did not work. The First World War transformed the place of women, as they took over many men's jobs. Its other legacies were the war memorials which joined the statues of Victorian worthies in main squares round the land. After 1918 death duties bit even harder and a quarter of England changed hands in a few years.

The multiple shop – the chain store – appeared in the high street: Sainsburys, Maypole, Lipton's, Home & Colonial, the Fifty Shilling Tailor, Burton, Boots, W.H. Smith. The shopper was spoilt for choice, attracted by the brash fascias and advertising hoardings for national brands like Bovril, Pears Soap, and Ovaltine. Many new buildings began to be seen, such as garages, motor showrooms, picture palaces (cinemas), 'palais de dance', and the bow-windowed, pebble-dashed, tile-hung, half-timbered houses that were built as ribbon-development along the roads and new bypasses or on the new estates nudging the green belts.

During the 1920s cars became more reliable and sophisticated as well as commonplace, with developments like the electric self-starter making them easier for women to drive. Who wanted to turn a crank handle in the new short skirt? This was, indeed, the electric age as much as the motor era. Trolley buses, electric trams and trains extended mass transport and electric light replaced gas in the street and the home, which itself was groomed by the vacuum cleaner.

Father and child cycling past Buckingham Palace on VE Day, 8 May 1945. (*Hulton Getty Picture Collection*)

A major jolt to the march onward and upward was administered by the Great Depression of the early 1930s. The older British industries – textiles, shipbuilding, iron, steel, coal – were already under pressure from foreign competition when this worldwide slump arrived, cutting exports by half in two years and producing 3 million unemployed (and still rising) by 1932. Luckily there were new diversions to alleviate the misery. The 'talkies' arrived in the cinemas; more and more radios and gramophones were to be found in people's homes; there were new women's magazines, with fashion, cookery tips and problem pages; football pools; the flying feats of women pilots like Amy Johnson; the Loch Ness Monster; cheap chocolate and the drama of Edward VIII's abdication.

Things were looking up again by 1936 and unemployment was down to 2 million. New light industry was booming in the Home Counties as factories struggled to keep up with the demand for radios, radiograms, cars and electronic goods including the first television sets. The threat from Hitler's Germany meant rearmament, particularly of the airforce, which stimulated aircraft and aero engine firms. If you were lucky and lived in the south, there was good money to be earned. A semi-detached house cost £450, a Morris Cowley £150. People may have smoked like chimneys but life expectancy, since 1918, was up by 15 years while the birth rate had almost halved. The fifty-four hour week was down to forty-eight hours and there were 9 million radio licences by 1939.

In some ways it is the little memories that seem to linger longest from the Second World War: the kerbs painted white to show up in the blackout, the rattle of ack-ack shrapnel on roof tiles, sparrows killed by bomb blast, painting your legs brown and then adding a black seam

A family gathered around their television set in the 1950s. (*Hulton Getty Picture Collection*)

down the back to simulate stockings. The biggest damage, apart from London, was in the south-west (Plymouth, Bristol) and the Midlands (Coventry, Birmingham). Postwar reconstruction was rooted in the Beveridge Report which set out the expectations for the Welfare State. This, together with the nationalisation of the Bank of England, coal, gas, electricity and the railways, formed the programme of the Labour government in 1945. At this time the USA was calling in its debts and Britain was beggared by the war, yet still administering its Empire.

Times were hard in the late 1940s, with rationing even more stringent than during the war. Yet this was, as has been said, 'an innocent and well-behaved era'. The first let-up came in 1951 with the Festival of Britain and then there was another fillip in 1953 from the Coronation, which incidentally gave a huge boost to the spread of TV. By 1954 leisure motoring had been resumed but the Comet – Britain's best hope for taking on the American aviation industry – suffered a series of mysterious crashes. The Suez debacle of 1956 was followed by an acceleration in the withdrawal from Empire, which had begun in 1947 with the Independence of India. Consumerism was truly born with the advent of commercial TV and most homes soon boasted washing machines, fridges, electric irons and fires.

The *Lady Chatterley* obscenity trial in 1960 was something of a straw in the wind for what was to follow in that decade. A collective loss of inhibition seemed to sweep the land, as stately home owners opened up, the Beatles and the Rolling Stones transformed popular music, and retailing, cinema and the theatre were revolutionised. Designers, hairdressers, photographers and models moved into places vacated by an Establishment put to flight by the new breed of satirists spawned by *Beyond the Fringe* and *Private Eye*.

In the 1970s Britain seems to have suffered a prolonged hangover after the excesses of the previous decade. Ulster, inflation and union troubles were not made up for by entry into the EEC, North Sea Oil, Women's Lib or, indeed, Punk Rock. Mrs Thatcher applied the corrective in the 1980s, as the country moved more and more from its old manufacturing base over to providing services, consulting, advertising, and expertise in the 'invisible' market of high finance or in IT. Britain entertained the world with *Cats*, *Phantom of the Opera*, *Four Weddings and a Funeral*, *The Full Monty*, *Mr Bean* and the *Teletubbies*.

The post-1945 townscape has seen changes to match those in the worlds of work, entertainment and politics. In 1956 the Clean Air Act served notice on smogs and pea-souper fogs, smuts and blackened buildings, forcing people to stop burning coal and go over to smokeless sources of heat and energy. In the same decade some of the best urban building took place in the 'new towns' like Basildon, Crawley, Stevenage and Harlow. Elsewhere open warfare was declared on slums and what was labelled inadequate, cramped, back-to-back, two-up, two-down, housing. The new 'machine for living in' was a flat in a high-rise block. The architects and planners who promoted these were in league with the traffic engineers, determined to keep the motor car moving whatever the price in multi-storey car parks, meters, traffic wardens and ring roads.

Carnaby Street in the 1960s. (*Barnaby's Picture Library*)

The Millennium Dome at Greenwich, 1999. (*Michael Durnan/Barnaby's Picture Library*)

The old pollutant, coal smoke, was replaced by petrol and diesel exhaust, and traffic noise. Even in the back garden it was hard to find peace as motor mowers, then leaf blowers and strimmers made themselves heard, and the neighbours let you share their choice of music from their powerful new amplifiers, whether you wanted to or not. Fast food was no longer only a pork pie in a pub or fish-and-chips. There were Indian curry houses, Chinese take-aways and American-style hamburgers, while the drinker could get away from beer in a wine bar. Under the impact of television the big Gaumonts and Odeons closed or were rebuilt as multi-screen cinemas, while the palais de dance gave way to discos and clubs.

From the late 1960s the introduction of listed buildings and conservation areas, together with the growth of preservation societies, put a brake on 'comprehensive redevelopment'. Now the new risk at the end of the 1990s is that town centres may die, as shoppers are attracted to the edge-of-town supermarkets surrounded by parking space, where much more than food and groceries can be bought. The ease of the one-stop shop represents the latest challenge to the good health of our towns. But with care, ingenuity and a determination to keep control of our environment, this challenge can be met.

Nottingham: An Introduction

The history of Nottingham in the twentieth century has perhaps not been as turbulent as in previous centuries but its citizens have lived through a period as exciting as any in the millennium.

The century has seen many notable successes and a few failures – the demolition of historic buildings being the greatest mistake.

Nottingham was created a city in 1897, which coincided with the Diamond Jubilee celebrations of Queen Victoria. In appearance it was a densely populated city with blackened Georgian and Victorian-style houses and public buildings.

The town had expanded rapidly in the nineteenth century, taking many of the surrounding suburbs within its boundaries and building on the land acquired after the passing of the Enclosure Act of 1845.

An alleyway lined with carcasses of meat in the Shambles behind the Exchange in 1921. The two men in the centre appear to be concluding a bargain. These butchers' stalls were unhygienic and the Corporation decided in the 1920s to demolish the whole area and build a new town hall and shopping arcade on the site.

The city authorities were aware of the need to clear away the insanitary slum properties in the inner city, particularly in the Broad Marsh area, but very little progress was made in this direction until after the First World War. In 1919 the Corporation made an attempt to enlarge the city's boundaries still further by acquiring the nearby towns, including Beeston, Arnold and West Bridgford. The Health Minister, however, was not impressed by the standard of housing in Nottingham and refused the application. This was a salutary shock for the city authorities and work commenced on the demolition of the condemned houses in Broad Marsh. At the same time, the building of council houses on new estates began and this was to continue until the late 1960s.

The Corporation's other great project in the 1920s was the building of the Council House. There had been plans for demolishing the old Exchange and constructing a new town hall from the middle of the nineteenth century but the cost involved was the obstacle. This was still the case in the years immediately after the First World War but, by this

The corner of Market Street and Upper Parliament Street before its demolition in 1928. The Three Crowns public house in the centre was rebuilt, but F.E. Barnett's outfitting shop made way for Martin's Bank, designed by T. Cecil Howitt. After the closure of the bank, this building became the Café Royal and is now O'Neill's, an Irish bar.

The skeleton of the Council House in 1927, appearing as a moon rocket ready for lift-off. After the small-scale Exchange, the new structure was overwhelming and it was some while before the people of Nottingham appreciated their new town hall. Although a public building, only a minority of citizens have been inside the Council House – for many years the building was not open to the public.

time, the Exchange was old-fashioned and the insalubrious meat stalls or Shambles behind the building were another blot on the city's reputation. The subsequent removal of the Goose Fair from the Market Place was a blow to the populace who feared that the fair would lose its appeal when transferred to the Forest.

The Council House was officially opened by the Prince of Wales on 22 May 1929 and, although this building is classical in design, Nottingham as a modern city may be said to date from this time. Nottingham folk, however, took some considerable time to appreciate the cleaner lines of the Old Market Square, as the Market Place was renamed, and it was quickly dubbed Slab Square.

The main industries of Nottingham until the end of the nineteenth century were lacemaking and knitwear but, coinciding with the decline of those trades, three new industries began in the town – these were to have a great impact both locally and nationally.

Jesse Boot, a local boy who began his career by helping his mother run her herbalist's shop in Goose Gate, went on to create the largest chain of chemist's shops in the country, together with the drug and toiletries factories to supply them.

John Player came to Nottingham from Saffron Walden and, after buying a small tobacco factory in Broad Marsh, created a major new industry which his two sons continued and enlarged. The trademark of Nottingham Castle on many packets of Players cigarettes ensured that the image of Nottingham went around the world. By the 1930s the company was one of the largest employers in the city and to work at Players was the ambition of many.

The third new industry of the late nineteenth century was the Raleigh Cycle Company. This was founded by Frank Bowden in 1887, after taking over a small cycle works, and by 1900 he had created the largest cycle factory in the world.

These three companies and others such as Ericsson's Telephones and a multitude of smaller and varied businesses buttressed Nottingham against the worst of the Depression between the two world wars.

Nottingham and its neighbour, Leicester, which had a similar population, enjoyed a friendly rivalry but Nottingham claimed to be the Queen of the Midlands and was proud of it. This rivalry surfaced when

A study in concentration at Sneinton Market in 1992. Women are choosing ribbons from a stall overflowing with haberdashery. Nottingham's markets are noted for their good value and attract citizens and visitors alike.

Nottingham's University College was looking for a site on which to build a new college. Sir Jesse Boot resolved to use his wealth to provide both the land and the money to build a new college for the East Midlands. Leicester was encouraged to participate in the scheme but the authorities decided to pursue their own plan to build a university college.

Nottingham's new University College was opened at Highfields on 10 July 1928 by King George V, the year the Mayor of Nottingham was given the title of Lord Mayor.

The interwar years, for the citizens of Nottingham, were not entirely devoted to work and study – the city had many varied leisure and entertainment outlets. Sportsmen and women who actively participated in their pursuits, were well provided for in the city – there were a number of swimming pools, bowling greens, tennis courts and sports fields. For those who preferred watching games, the two local football teams, Nottingham Forest and Notts. County, while never winning any major trophies in the 1920s and 1930s, were well supported. The Nottinghamshire County Cricket Club, which staged Test Matches attracting large crowds, had several England players in their team, of whom Larwood and Voce were the most famous.

Nottingham, like all industrial cities, had numerous public houses, many of them famous for their age and associations, such as the Trip to Jerusalem and the Salutation. This was also the period when cafés abounded and Nottingham people with long memories will recall the Mikado, Kardomah, Lloyds, the Oriental and Lyon's, many of which were famous for their confectionery.

This was the golden age of cinema – every district had at least one – and there were several in the Nottingham city centre including the Scala, Hippodrome, Mechanics and Elite, all of which have now closed. The Ritz – now the Odeon – and the Carlton, renamed ABC Cinemas, were both built in the 1930s on the site of old property in the Mount Street area of the city.

Dancing was another pastime of the interwar years. The Palais de Danse which, after becoming Ritzy's night club, has now been reincarnated as the Palais, was noted for its tea-dances. Other well-known halls of the period were the Greyfriars Ballroom, now the MGM Nightclub, and the Victoria Ballroom, later the Locarno.

When the Second World War began, the population was lulled into a false sense of security by the inactivity on the battlefields of France. From 1940 onwards, however, Nottingham – like other industrial cities – was under threat from German air attacks. The city suffered only one major blitz, in May 1941, when 159 people were killed and considerable damage was caused. The long war was very taxing although the comradeship of the population was notable and helped in the postwar years of austerity.

During the war, plans were made for a civic centre to be built north of Shakespeare Street but this never came to fruition. However, in the 1950s, the scheme which was to cause the greatest controversy was conceived. This was the construction of Maid Marian Way, through one of the oldest parts of Nottingham, replacing some of the city's finest buildings with multi-storey structures of no architectural merit. Parts of the Lace Market also suffered from demolition – a number of Victorian lace warehouses were pulled down before the city authorities realised that an important part of Nottingham's heritage was being destroyed.

The 1960s was another decade of thoughtless destruction of historic buildings, including the Black Boy Hotel, Victoria Railway Station and Drury Hill – the last two in the construction of the city's two main shopping centres.

Following the protests over the loss of such important assets to Nottingham, the Corporation began to take more notice of public opinion.

Twentieth-century Nottingham, unlike the town in previous centuries, has not played a major role in national affairs, but sporting achievements have brought attention to the city. In the 1970s and 1980s Nottingham Forest, by winning the Football League Championship and the European Cup twice under the management of Brian Clough, showed outstanding abilities. The Nottinghamshire County Cricket Club, with Richard Hadlee and Clive Rice in the team, won the Britannic Assurance Championship and the NatWest Trophy in 1987. Perhaps the greatest achievement in Nottingham sport was the ice-dance success of Jayne Torvill and Christopher Dean in the 1980s and '90s, which captured the attention of the city and the whole nation.

All Britain's cities attempt to create a good image of themselves and Nottingham is no exception. Its boast of being the regional capital has to be sustained for it to attract Government organisations and major companies to the city. The regeneration of the land adjoining the Nottingham Canal has made a significant improvement in the landscape of that area. Further east, on the old Boots Island Street site, developments are taking place which will hopefully bring life to that district.

The building of the new National Ice Centre on the site of the old Ice Stadium is possibly the most exciting development in the city at the turn of the century, although the construction of a tram system planned for the new millennium is also eagerly awaited.

At the end of a hundred years of considerable change for the city, and as we prepare for a new century, the citizens of Nottingham can look back with pride at their achievements.

Edwardian Nottingham

Middle Marsh, *c.* 1893. To the right is Narrow Marsh, also known as Red Lion Street, and straight ahead is Garners Hill, previously named Brightmore Hill. This was the most densely populated area in the city and this junction was at its centre. Middleton's drug store on the left advertises single articles at wholesale prices. On the skyline is the High Pavement Unitarian Chapel, then the tallest building in Nottingham.

Workmen re-laying the cobbles in the road at the foot of Market Street, *c.* 1890. Men at work have always drawn onlookers and this is no exception. In those days this task was almost entirely manual; steamrollers and steam shovels were only beginning to make an appearance on major projects. Market Street was the first wide road to be constructed leading north out of the Market Place. When it was built in 1865 it was originally called Theatre Street but, unaccountably, the public were affronted by this name and it was quickly renamed Market Street.

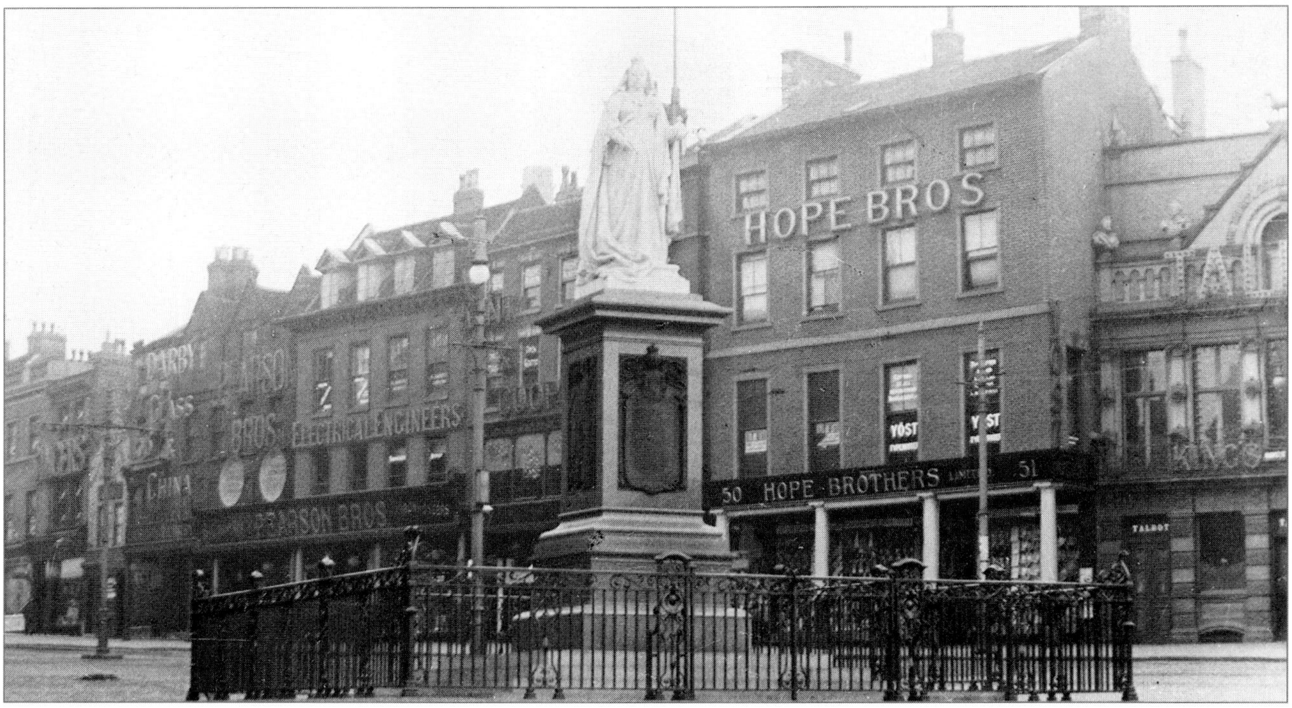

The statue of Queen Victoria had pride of place at the west end of the Market Place in 1910. In the background, on Long Row West, are a number of well-known shops, including Singer's Sewing Machines, Darby's glass and china store, Pearson Bros, Kent and Cooper's music shop and Hope Brothers, clothiers. On the right is the Talbot, a flamboyant drinking palace, and the King's Theatre.

The memorial to the dead of the Boer War at the junction of King Street and Queen Street in 1910. This was the gift of T.I. Birkin, lace manufacturer, and was unveiled in 1903. On the left is the General Post Office and to the right is the Prudential Assurance building, designed by Alfred Waterhouse. The war memorial was removed to a site on the Forest in 1927 when a trolley bus terminus was placed here.

Mansfield Road, viewed from Trinity Square in 1897. This is the main road to the north from Nottingham and was built up in the late nineteenth century. The buildings on the right were all scheduled for demolition in preparation for the construction of the Victoria Railway Station. On the immediate right is one of Marsden's earliest grocery stores and the shop next to it is advertising a closing-down sale.

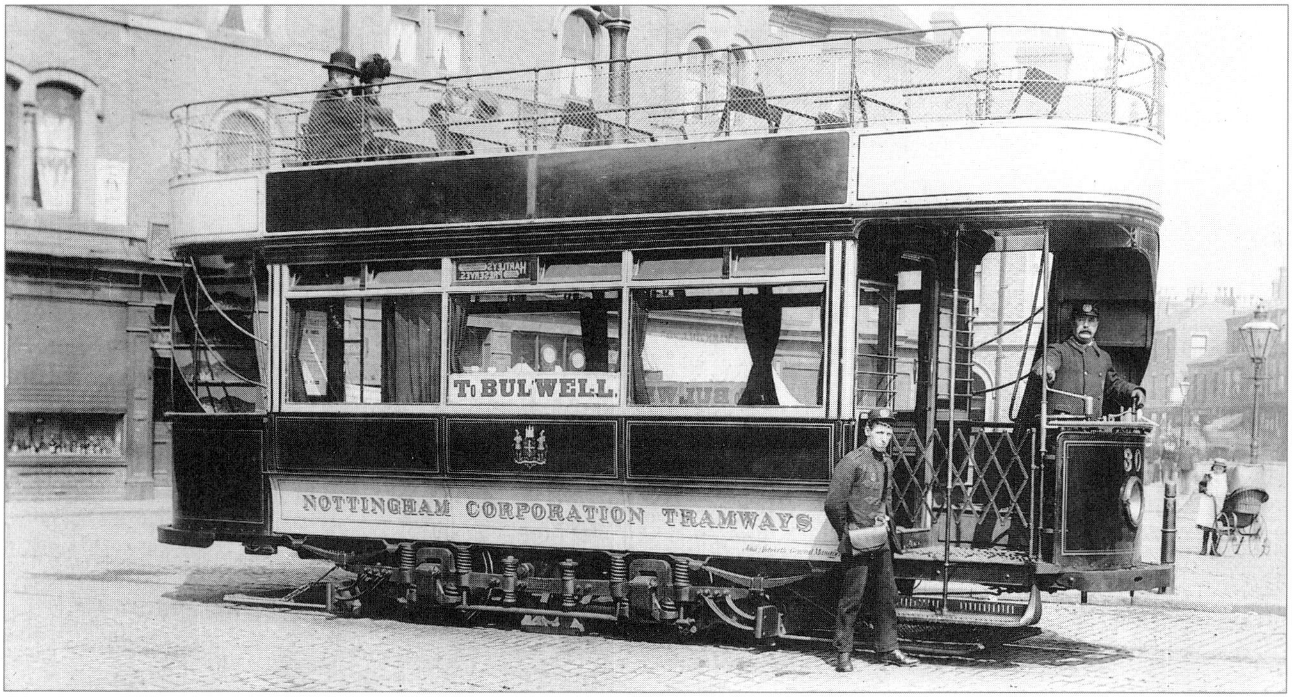

An electric tram at its terminus in Bulwell Market Place in 1901. The driver is George Langsdale who previously drove horse trams on this route. From their introduction onto the streets of Nottingham in that year, electric trams were a great success and horse trams were unable to compete with them.

The first bus owned by Barton Bros, with Kate Barton at the wheel in 1908. The bus, which was a 28 horse-power Durham Churchill, carried twenty-eight people and was en route from Long Eaton to the Goose Fair. The bus continued in service until 1918 and was later rebuilt on a Daimler chassis and used for publicity purposes and charity events.

The Lambert family with a de Dion Voiturette automobile outside the family home, Ellesmere House on Clarendon Street, *c.* 1900. Mabel and Dudley Lambert watch as their parents and a friend prepare to drive away. The Lamberts, whose business was lace dressing, were a wealthy and philanthropic family who played a leading role in Nottingham's civic affairs.

The Nottingham Fire Brigade practising in the drill yard of the Guildhall in 1912. The appliance on the left is one of the Dennis motor fire appliances which the brigade acquired in 1911, capable of delivering 500 to 800 gallons of water a minute. On the right is a Shand & Mason steam fire-engine which had been in service for almost half a century.

Five young girls and one boy pose for a photograph for the family album *c.* 1900 – all dressed in their Sunday best clothes, the girls with wide-brimmed hats. They are all very composed apart from the young lady sitting on the mat in the middle, who has become bored with the proceedings and apparently fallen asleep.

John Lambert singing to the accompaniment of his daughter Mabel, at his home – Ellesmere House, *c.* 1900. The Victorians enjoyed home entertainments in the evenings and all affluent families were proficient at the keyboard. The Lamberts were also enthusiastic photographers and recorded all their activities for their family album.

Spring-cleaning at Blenheim House, St Ann's Hill, *c.* 1900 – the domestic staff vigorously beating and brushing the upholstery in the annual ritual. This was the home of Albert Armitage whose company owned a number of grocery stores and several cafés, including the Mikado on Long Row and the Oriental in Wheeler Gate.

General William Booth arriving in the City of London in 1905 to receive the Freedom of the City. Born in Notintone Place, Sneinton, in 1829, he started attending the Broad Street Wesleyan Chapel when he was fifteen and shortly afterwards began his evangelistic work which he continued until his death in 1912.

Sir John Rees addressing a meeting in Sneinton Market during the by-election in the Nottingham East constituency in 1912. The crowd is composed almost entirely of men who, with the exception of Sir John, are all wearing hats or caps – the fashion of the time.

An election rally held by Sir John Rees in a factory yard near St Ann's Well Road in 1912. Some women are in evidence in this crowd, wearing long full dresses in dark colours with hats to match. Sir John, a Conservative and Unionist, won the election with a majority of 1,324. He died after falling from an express train in 1922.

Goose Fair in the Market Place in 1914. The Big Wheel, which appears to be of the frailest construction, is in a prime position, next to the statue of Queen Victoria. Behind the wheel is the Cake-Walk, a recent import from America and very popular.

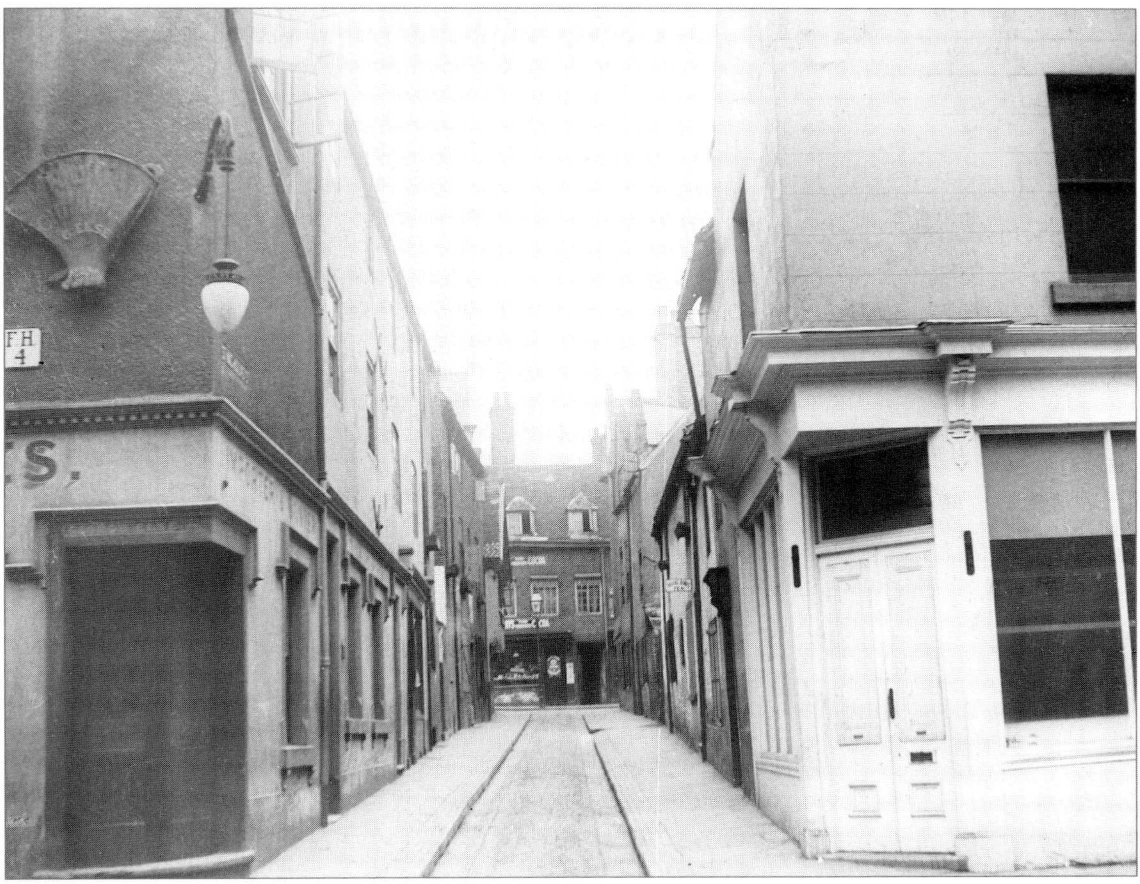

St Nicholas Street looking towards Hounds Gate in 1910. The building on the left is the Royal Children, a seventeenth-century inn which was demolished in the 1930s and rebuilt in mock-Tudor style. The whalebone hanging over the door was a relic from the days when the inn sold whale-oil for lamps. The bone is now preserved in a glass case in one of the bars.

The Picture House in 1912, the year the building was converted into a cinema. This was one of the earliest cinemas in the city and it was quickly followed by others. In the 1940s, at the height of picture-going, there were over thirty cinemas in Nottingham. This cinema closed in 1930 when Lyons, which had previously been next door, acquired the building and opened a café.

The First World War and the 1920s

The statue of Captain Albert Ball VC in the Nottingham Castle grounds. One of the great flying aces of the First World War, he was credited with the destruction of at least forty-four enemy planes. He was shot down in 1917 at the age of twenty, shortly after receiving the Freedom of the City of Nottingham. The statue is the work of the sculptor Henry Poole.

Captain Albert Ball VC in the cockpit of an SES A4850 fighter-plane in 1917. At the beginning of the First World War he enlisted in the Sherwood Foresters and later transferred to the Royal Flying Corps.

The official party at the unveiling of the statue of Captain Albert Ball VC in the Castle grounds, 1921. In the front row from the left are Col A.W. Brewill DSO, Robin Hood Battalion of the Sherwood Foresters; Alderman A. Ball; Mrs Ball and W.J. Board, Town Clerk. Back row: Mrs Bowles, Mayoress; Air Marshal Sir Hugh Trenchard; H. Bowles, Mayor; J.H. Freckingham, Sheriff, and Mrs Freckingham.

The corner of Lister Gate and Castle Gate after the Zeppelin raid on Nottingham on 23 September 1916. The main damage was to premises in Greyfriar Gate but J.H. Haywood's factory on the right suffered some damage as did houses in the Meadows. Haywood's factory was badly damaged in the blitz on Nottingham in the Second World War and had to be evacuated.

Houses in Newthorpe Street destroyed in the Zeppelin raid in 1916. Although most Nottingham people were aware of the raid, publication of the news was withheld until 1919.

Women window-cleaners on Long Row East in 1917. In the First World War women replaced men in a number of occupations such as tram conductresses, munition workers, farm-hands and mechanics. Boots the Chemists in the background are advertising 'Presents for the Troops'. Sir Jesse Boot was a great patriot and he began a newsletter 'Comrades in Khaki' for company employees serving abroad.

A woman postal worker collecting mail from the letter-box at the foot of Market Street in 1916. In the background is a fashion display in one of Griffin & Spalding's windows.

The Market Place on Armistice Day, 11 November 1918. The parade consisted mainly of civilians with some troops and personnel from the auxiliary services. The end of the war was not unexpected but, with the appalling casualties suffered by all the nations involved, the general mood was of joy and relief.

Two soldiers drinking beer outside Lyon's Café, Long Row, on Armistice Day, 1918. They could be forgiven for indulging themselves but doubtless they had help in emptying these bottles.

Women at a well in Clifton in 1923. Until 1933 when the village was connected to Nottingham's water system, the only source of water for Clifton was a number of pumps and wells and the water carriers who visited the outlying cottages. The village pumps and wells were meeting places for the local inhabitants, where news and gossip were exchanged.

A vintage motor car crossing the Wilford Toll Bridge in 1922. The bridge opened in 1870 and was regularly used by Nottingham people on outings to Wilford and Clifton, and also by the occasional vehicle and herd of sheep. The board above the turnstile, which still exists, itemises the tolls payable for the various categories of vehicles and animals crossing the bridge. In 1974 the bridge was closed to motor traffic and to all traffic in 1981 when it was rebuilt for pedestrians and cyclists only.

A gypsy encampment on waste land at Bulwell in the 1920s. These camps were a familiar sight in those days and, although perhaps not welcome, they were tolerated. A purchase from a gypsy woman who called at your home with pegs or bunches of heather was deemed necessary to prevent an evil spell being cast.

A row of houses at Plantation Side, Bobbers Mill, 1922. These were known as Moseley's Buildings and were built in the nineteenth century to house workers at the nearby mills and bleach works on the River Leen.

The Prince of Wales being welcomed by employees while visiting Boots Island Street factories in August 1923. On the left is the Mayor, Alderman Edward Manning and on the right is John Boot, vice-chairman of Boots. Sir Jesse Boot was still nominally the chairman of the company but, crippled as he was with arthritis, he was unable to be present during the Prince's visit.

Boots soap works at Beeston in 1928. This was the first automated production line at the new site and here girls are seen packing Kudos Soap Flakes. Sir Jesse Boot's dream was to build a garden factory similar to Port Sunlight and Bournville but it was left to his son to achieve this ambition.

A group of *Nottingham Evening Post* workers in Burton Street in the 1920s studying the back page of the newspaper they had helped to produce. Presumably the sports page was more interesting than the front page whose headline read 'MPs whistle the Dead March in all-night sitting'. Unfortunately this tantalising piece of news from the House of Commons is not very enlightening.

T.E. Lawrence (Lawrence of Arabia) on a Brough Superior motorcycle with the maker George Brough at his Vernon Road factory. These machines were the Rolls-Royce of motorcycles and T.E. Lawrence owned seven during his life. He had an eighth on order when he was killed riding one in 1935.

The traditional opening ceremony of Goose Fair at the bottom of Market Street in 1925. The Town Clerk, Sir William Board, is reading the proclamation of the granting of the charter and, to his right, is the Mayor, Charles Foulds, who was to perform the opening ceremony. This would be followed by the Mayor's party making a tour of the fair, riding on 'the Horses' and returning to the Exchange with arms full of prizes.

The front of John Proctor's Royal Circus at the Goose Fair, *c.* 1920. Proctor's were fairground entertainers of long-standing and owned roundabouts as well as side-shows. Almost the entire troupe seems to be on the platform in front of the tent, including a military band, Scottish pipers, clowns, acrobats and a Red Indian Chief.

The re-laying of the tramlines in the Old Market Square in 1929, when the square was being redesigned after the open-air market had been removed. The trams were to remain for another seven years only before being replaced by trolley buses. On the left is Griffin & Spalding's new department store, and other well-known names on Long Row are the Mikado Café, Lyons Café, Lipton's stores and Samuel's the jewellers.

The Fish, Game and Poultry Market in King Edward Street in 1929 – the year in which it opened. In the left foreground are Ford's, who had then been established for over a century. Neither traders nor customers were initially pleased with the relocation of the market but they gradually became reconciled to it.

ALEXANDRES
CAFE
SAVOY
ALLCOCK & CO.
A. & P. LAKE
A & P. LAKE

Wheeler Gate, 1929. The main road to the south from the Old Market Square was almost always congested with traffic. In this photograph there are a variety of vehicles, including a horse-drawn trap, a railway dray, a man on a tricycle with a milk-churn, pedal and motor-cycles and a number of splendid motor cars. On the left are two adjoining cafés, the Savoy and Morley's and on the right is the Canadian Fur Company – all now closed.

Park Steps in 1928. This steep slope leading down from The Ropewalk to Park Valley was the ancient route from Nottingham to Lenton. These steps were first cut in the 1820s when the Duke of Newcastle began to develop the castle park. The Park still remains an oasis of calm and is unique in English town planning.

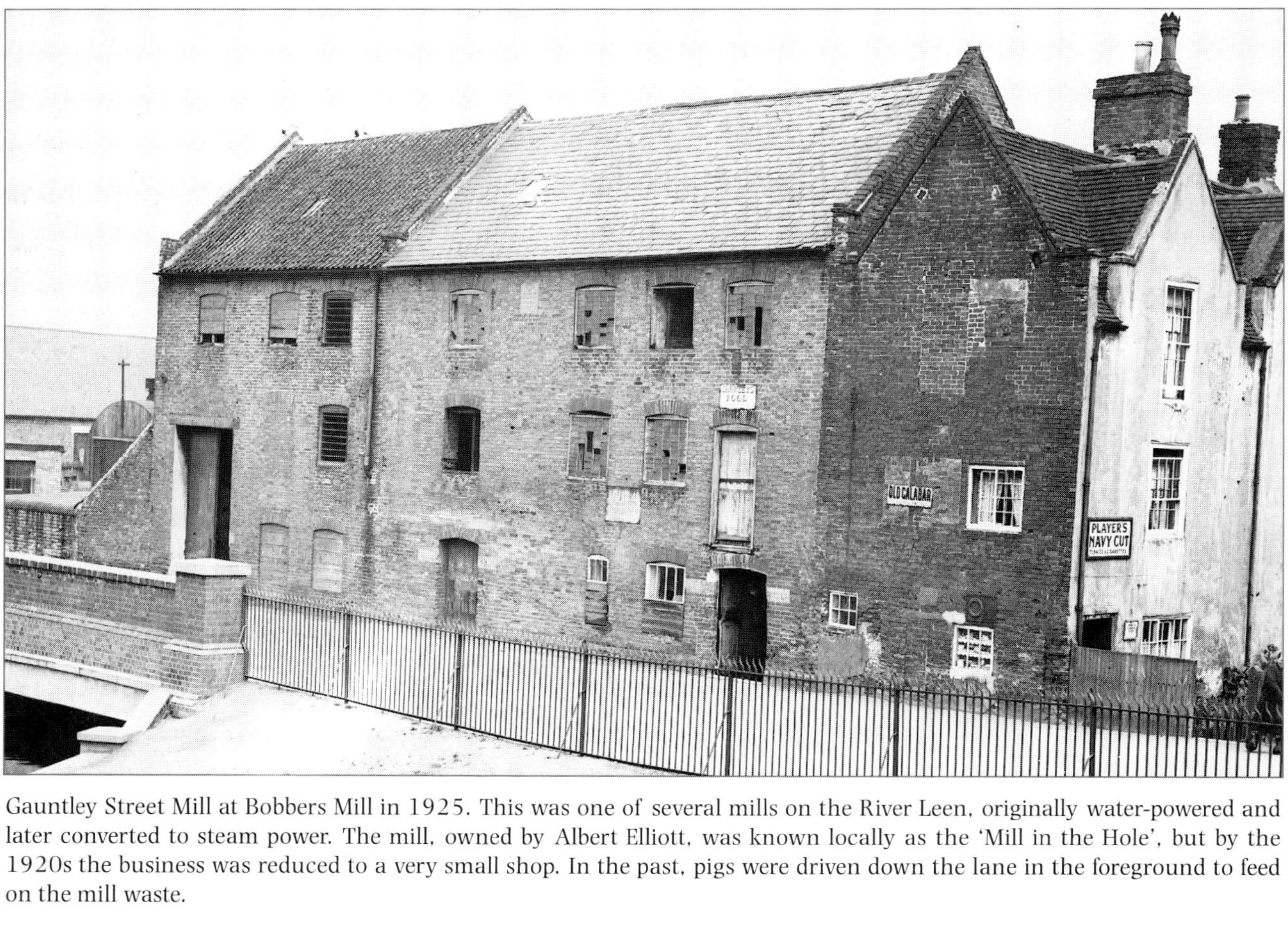

Gauntley Street Mill at Bobbers Mill in 1925. This was one of several mills on the River Leen, originally water-powered and later converted to steam power. The mill, owned by Albert Elliott, was known locally as the 'Mill in the Hole', but by the 1920s the business was reduced to a very small shop. In the past, pigs were driven down the lane in the foreground to feed on the mill waste.

Sussex Street in 1928 looking towards Broad Marsh. At the corner of Harrington Street is James Stevenson's butcher's shop and adjoining it is William Jerram's pork butcher's shop. This street and Broad Marsh were the main shopping streets of a very congested area, which was by this date already condemned.

Garibaldi Yard, also known as Cave Chambers, off Bridlesmith Gate in 1921. The house on the left was one of the few Elizabethan buildings left in Nottingham and had caves beneath it which were reputedly haunted. The house was demolished in 1933 when the area was redeveloped.

ME MAKER
OMMERCIAL
AND
HOTEL
HEAD
SPIRITS
MILTON ST

The busy junction of Milton Street and Parliament Street in 1929. Trams were still running down the centre of Nottingham's roads but pedestrians jay-walked in front of them with little concern. A white-coated policeman at the junction of the roads is attempting to assert his authority. The Milton's Head Hotel – a solid Victorian building – appeared to be a permanent fixture but it was demolished when the Victoria Shopping Centre was built.

Ruston's Place, off Bellar Gate, 1919. These were some of the infamous back-to-back houses which blighted Nottingham's reputation in the early twentieth century. The yards between the houses were the only areas where daylight reached and it was here that women washed their clothes, children played and neighbours gossiped.

The 1930s

Carrington Street in 1930 when this road led straight to the Midland Railway Station. On the right is The James Store, a well-known drapery emporium of that period and, at the corner of Broad Marsh, is the cupola of Montague Burton's – the tailors. Breaking the skyline are the spires of St Peter's Church and Holy Trinity Church and the dome of the newly-built Council House. The traffic is fairly light with the slow-moving horse-drawn vehicles keeping to the inner lane. The leading motor car is a Morris Cowley followed by a 20 horse power Rolls-Royce.

Boots General Offices on Station Street in 1930. This was originally Hine & Mundella's steam-powered hosiery factory built in 1851 by T.C. Hine. Jesse Boot began to lease rooms in the factory in 1908 and purchased the whole building in 1912. As he expanded his business he acquired more property in the area and began his own printing works. The General Offices were closed down in 1968 and the building was demolished four years later.

The architectural masterpiece designed by Sir Owen Williams for Boots in the early 1930s. John Boot, the second Lord Trent, continued the work begun by his father in expanding the company and making use of technological advances. The production lines of this factory at Beeston were completely automated with workers sitting at conveyor belts checking and packing products. In 1991 this factory, known prosaically as D.10 or the Wets factory, was completely refurbished.

Boots premier store in the city in 1933. This shop on the corner of Pelham Street, the second owned by Boots on this site, was built in 1903 to a design by Albert Bromley, an architect widely used by Jesse Boot. Many new departments were included in the store such as gift and book sections, a library and later a café. These additions were the result of the influence of Jesse's wife, Florence. This shop became a model for many stores which Boots opened in other towns and cities in the early years of the twentieth century. This branch was closed in 1972 when the new Boots shop in the Victoria Shopping Centre was opened.

Boots Day and Night branch, Wheeler Gate in 1934 – a Nottingham institution until it closed in 1962. The shop, which opened in 1917, was extended and given a new fascia in 1933. Like all Boots shops of the time, the windows were filled from top to bottom with items for sale – from patent medicines to toiletries and gifts.

Boots Typists' Training Bureau in 1936. Boots opened a Day Continuation School in 1920 for students who were taught initially English and mathematics. In 1935 a department for the tuition of shorthand and typewriting was opened and was to continue until 1984. The typewriters the girls are using are different models – Smith, Remington, Royal and Imperial – but the students look far more uniform than they would today.

Girls learning to embroider at Boots College, Beeston, *c.* 1935. Young employees were given tuition one day a week in a variety of subjects including art, music, English language and literature, French, geography, singing, cookery and dancing. The college closed after fifty years in 1969.

The University College, Highfields Park, in 1935. The college set on a hill overlooking the Trent Valley was the dream of Sir Jesse Boot in the last decade of his life. After acquiring this land in 1919 with the idea of building a garden factory and model village, ill health forced him to sell his company. It was then that the idea of using Highfields for a new university college was suggested to him and he put all his energy and a considerable amount of money into the scheme.

The bust of Lord Trent, as Sir Jesse Boot became in 1929, in front of the University College at Highfields. The inscription reads 'Our great citizen, Jesse Boot, Lord Trent. Before him lies a monument to his industry. Behind, an everlasting monument to his benevolence'.

A local inhabitant viewing the remains of the houses in Red Lion Street, otherwise known as Narrow Marsh, in 1933. These houses had been condemned as uninhabitable for a number of years and were finally being pulled down. Many of the dwellings were lodging houses and overcrowding was commonplace. In the background is St Patrick's Church which was to remain until 1979.

Workmen bricking up some of the caves discovered at the rear of the houses in Red Lion Street when they were demolished in 1933. Almost all the houses had caves cut out of the sandstone, used in the past for storage, brewing or tanning. In recent years some of the caves in Broad Marsh have been re-opened as a tourist attraction.

The Windmill Inn at the corner of Pilcher Gate and Fletcher Gate in 1930. This public house was once known as the Four Coffins and later as the Crown and Cushion. Pilcher Gate was named after the pilchers or furriers in the street, and Fletcher Gate, formerly Blowbladder Street, after the fleshers or butchers who lived and worked here. The public house was closed in 1971 when redevelopment was taking place in the area.

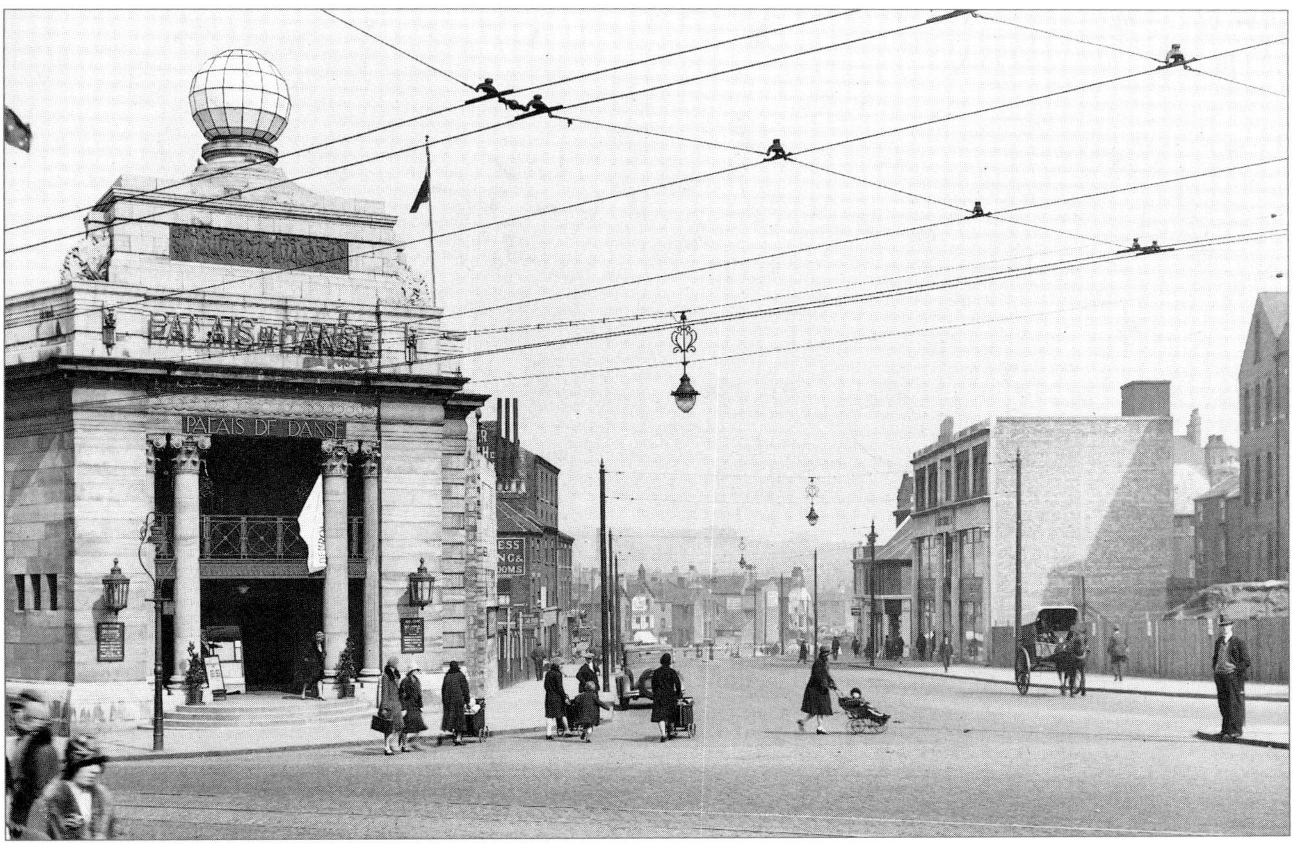

Lower Parliament Street in 1930, then being extended to Carter Gate. The Palais de Danse, built in 1925 in art deco style on the site of the old House of Correction, was the last word in dance halls. When it was first opened, advertisements advised that evening dress was essential and carriages were to be ordered for 1.30 a.m. The interior of the Palais, as it is now named, has been entirely renovated with many of the original features restored.

The Nottinghamshire versus Lancashire cricket match at Trent Bridge in 1932, viewed from the Pavilion Long Room. Both these teams were strong contenders for the County Championship title and the match was well attended. Nottinghamshire's batting strength was such that they fielded an entire team of players who had scored a century of runs.

The huge crowd at Trent Bridge for the England versus Australia Test Match in June 1938. In those days spectators were allowed to spill onto the pitch, although viewing was difficult for them. The match was notable for an innings of 232 in just over three hours by the Australian Stan McCabe while seven wickets fell at the other end.

Tom Blower, the Nottingham swimmer, on the left, being welcomed ashore at Dover after swimming the English Channel in 1937. His time for the crossing from Cap Gris Nez to Dover was 13 hours 29 minutes and in 1948 he swam the Channel in the reverse direction. In 1947 he was the first man to swim the North Channel – making the crossing from Donaghadee to Portpatrick in 15 hours 26 minutes.

Two water-skiers skimming over the water, making a series of V-shapes, near Trent Bridge in 1939.

Decorations for the Coronation of King George VI and Queen Elizabeth being prepared outside Burton's shop, Smithy Row, May 1937. Children were given a day's holiday from school for the event and all received a commemorative mug.

The crowded Central Market festooned with flags and bunting for the Coronation of King George VI and Queen Elizabeth in 1937. The flower and plant stalls of the market were always a blaze of colour and on this occasion they were even more colourful than usual.

The Second World War and the Postwar Years

A horse-drawn bus borrowed from the Leicester Corporation to celebrate the Golden Jubilee of the Nottingham Corporation Transport Department in 1948. The fare for the journey from the Walter Fountain to Lenton was 1*s* and most of the passengers seem to prefer the top deck for the ride. The Walter Fountain was built in 1866 to commemorate John Walter MP, the proprietor of *The Times*, and remained here until 1950 when it was removed as part of a new road scheme.

A decontamination squad at Boots Island Street Works, 1940. During the Second World War all companies took precautions against air attacks and major firms had fire-fighters on their premises. These terrifying-looking men are practising for a gas attack which fortunately never came.

The devastated University College on Shakespeare Street after the German blitz on Nottingham on 8/9 May 1941. This was the worst air raid of the war on the city and will never be forgotten by those who experienced it. Nottingham was fortunate and did not suffer any other major raids but 181 people were killed in total. The college was rebuilt after the war in a style similar to that of the original building.

A bomb crater on the pitch at the Trent Bridge cricket ground after the German air raid of May 1941. Although this damage was relatively unimportant, many major buildings were destroyed in the raid, including the Moot Hall, the Registry Office and several churches. The day after the raid there was a pervading smell of burning in the air and whole areas of the city were cordoned off.

Bomb damage at the Notts. County Football Club ground at Meadow Lane after the enemy air raid of May 1941. Fortunately, only light structural damage was caused here but 49 people lost their lives at the nearby Nottingham Co-operative Society Dairy, which received a direct hit.

The Old Market Square crowded with people celebrating VE Day, 8 May 1945. The time was 3 p.m. when Winston Churchill was broadcasting to the nation – a speech relayed throughout the square. Armistice Day and VE Day were both days when citizens showed their relief and joy at the ending of an horrific war. Crowds stayed in the centre of Nottingham until almost midnight – dancing, listening to music and just talking.

A street party in Back Cottages, Commercial Road, Bulwell on VE Day. This was one of many parties which were held in Nottingham at the end of the Second World War. Bunting and flags were quickly brought down from lofts and food such as jelly, trifle and cakes were miraculously produced to the delight of children who had rarely seen such fare before.

Nottingham folk fascinated by a German midget submarine on display with other captured enemy weapons in the Old Market Square, October 1945. The submarine, which was called a Beaver, was not a suicide weapon and carried torpedoes on each side of the hull.

An Avro Lancaster bomber, one of several aircraft on display on the Forest in September 1948. The Lancaster, powered by four Rolls-Royce Merlin engines, was the mainstay of Britain's air offensive against Germany during the Second World War. The children climbing into the aeroplane were able to experience the claustrophobic atmosphere in the fuselage and the feeling of exposure in the gun turrets.

A fair held in Bridgford Park, West Bridgford, on 10 August 1945, three days before the surrender of the Japanese to the allies. During the war, citizens were encouraged to take holidays at home and events like this fair were regularly arranged. Although most people were reduced to wearing old and shabby clothes by the end of the war, some – as in this photograph – were able to look elegant with limited means.

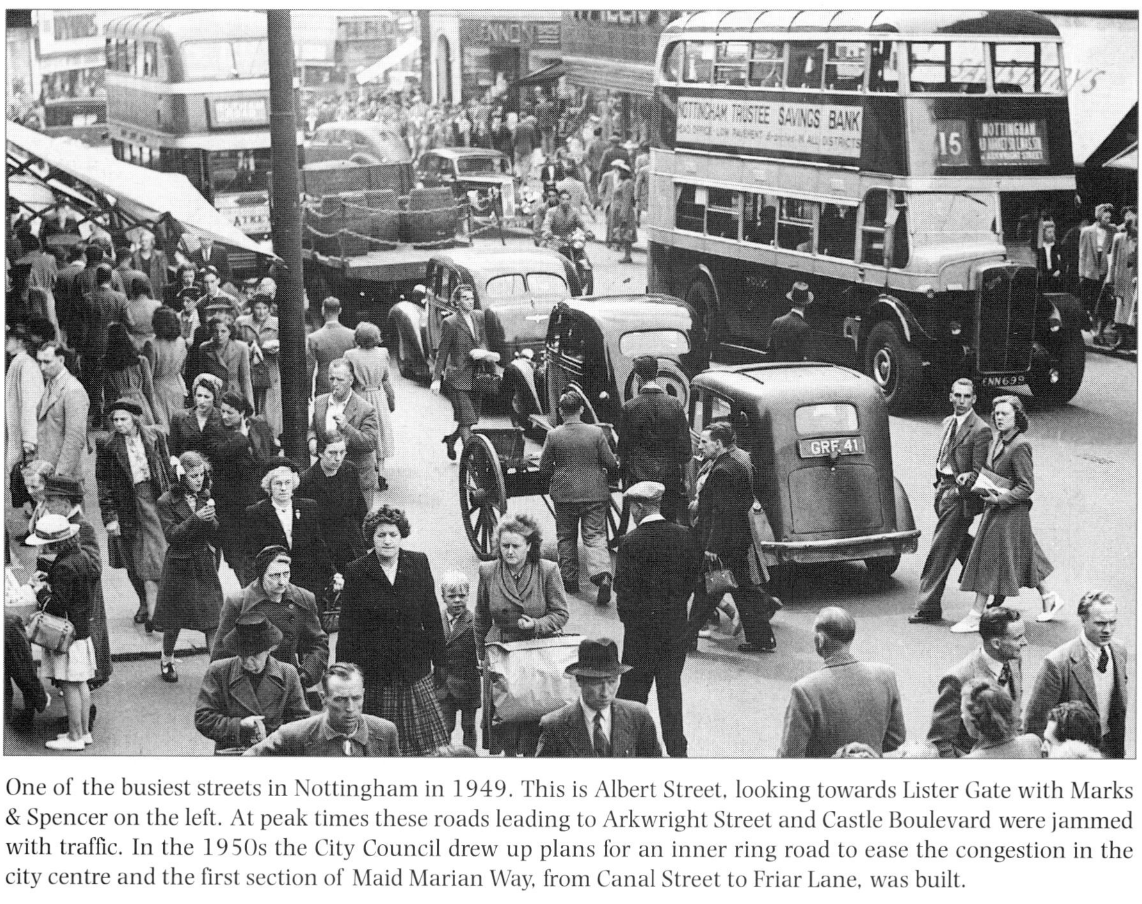

One of the busiest streets in Nottingham in 1949. This is Albert Street, looking towards Lister Gate with Marks & Spencer on the left. At peak times these roads leading to Arkwright Street and Castle Boulevard were jammed with traffic. In the 1950s the City Council drew up plans for an inner ring road to ease the congestion in the city centre and the first section of Maid Marian Way, from Canal Street to Friar Lane, was built.

Sunshine on the cobbles of the Old Market Square in January 1947, beautifying an ordinary scene. In the shadow of Beastmarket Hill are the Fifty Shilling Tailors and also the King's Restaurant – one of several well-known cafés in the city centre.

An earnest discussion in the Old Market Square in 1948. Fred Stone, in the right foreground, was a regular orator in the square for over fifty years and would revile his audience – having no brief for the orthodox church. Among the crowd are several Mormons and John Peck, the communist, facing the camera, who later became a city councillor.

Willing supporters helping to clear the snow from the Nottingham Forest football ground in March 1947. This was a harsh winter with record falls of snow followed by heavy rain which caused widespread flooding. The football season was extended into June because of the number of postponed matches.

A train running at slow speed through the flooded Midland Railway Station in March 1947. These floods – the last major floods in the city – caused widespread disruption in the Meadows and West Bridgford. Since then, the flood defence barriers along the River Trent have prevented a repetition of these scenes.

Families, marooned in their upper floors by the floods of March 1947, getting supplies in a novel way.

Two men canoeing down Jennison Street, Bulwell, during the floods of 1947, while local residents point out the danger of the snow still remaining in the water.

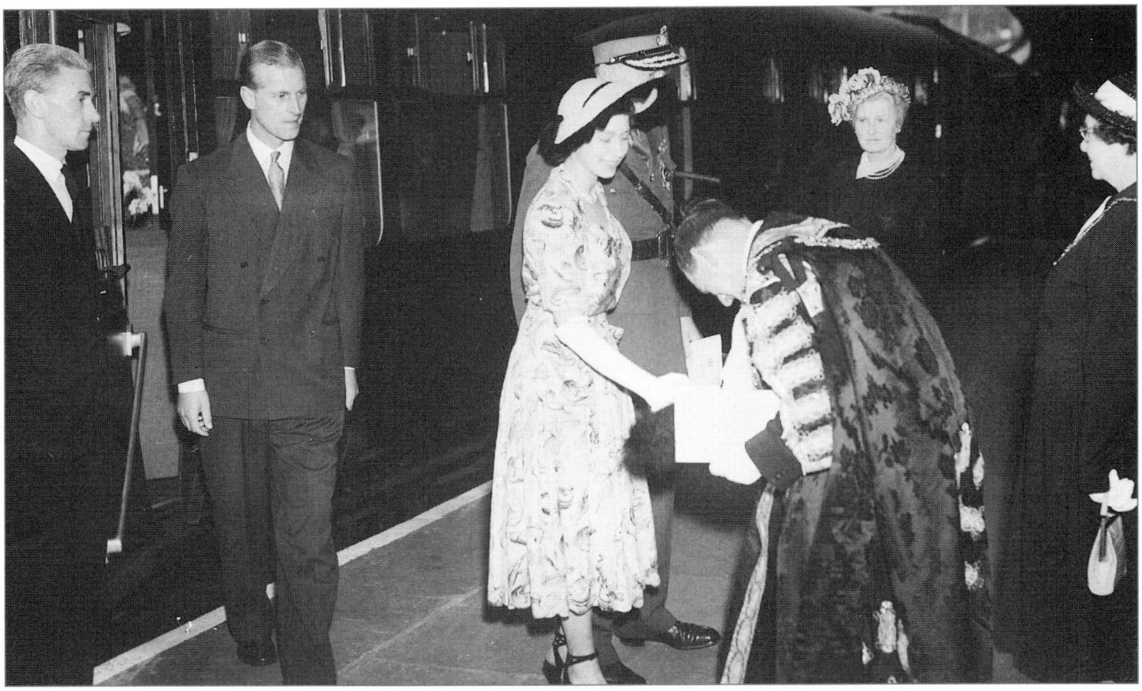

The Lord Mayor, Alderman W. Sharp, welcoming Princess Elizabeth and the Duke of Edinburgh at the Victoria Railway Station in June 1949. The city was commemorating the five hundredth anniversary of the granting of the Great Charter to the borough by Henry VI, thereby making the town a county in its own right.

Princess Elizabeth and the Duke of Edinburgh arriving in the Old Market Square for the official welcome during their visit for the Quincentenary. Many events were held during the summer of 1949, including a trades exhibition on Queens Drive, concerts, athletic events, water sports, pageants and fireworks.

The 1950s

Carlton Street, looking towards Goose Gate in 1958. On the left is J. & H. Bell, a well-known firm of printers and stationers, and beyond is the George Hotel, one of the oldest hotels in the city. Many famous people have stayed here, including Charles Dickens and Henry Irving. Goose Gate was then a busy shopping street attracting customers from Sneinton and beyond. After a period of decline this area has now been revived.

Members of the Mothers' Club at the Sycamore Community Centre celebrating Shrove Tuesday with a pancake race round the centre in Lilac Street. One of the rules was that the contestants should toss their pancakes at each street corner. A slip on these cobbles would see the end of a competitor's chance of winning the race.

The Nottingham Operatic Society celebrated its sixtieth anniversary in 1953 with a dinner-dance followed by excerpts from the shows performed during those years. Donald Timmins, the musical director, is going through a score with some of the principals of the society at the dress rehearsal.

Crowning the Clifton May Queen in 1953. Patricia Bowers is being crowned by her predecessor and attendant, Sheila Butler, while local children give their support.

Part of the Notts. and Derbys. Salvation Army Young People's Coronation Pageant at the Albert Hall in 1953. This tableau represents the community of nations with all the participants wearing national costumes.

The Lord Mayor, Councillor L.H. Willson chatting with some of the cubs after he had taken the salute at the St George's Day Parade in the Old Market Square in 1953. This parade, attended by all the local voluntary organisations is, like many other events of this period, now discontinued.

Mr Justice Finnemore inspecting the guard of honour of the Boys Brigade at the service at St Mary's Church, before the opening of the Nottinghamshire Assizes in 1953. These church services, which are of ancient origin, continued to be held until 1994. The Assizes have now been transferred from the Shire Hall to the new Crown Courts on Canal Street.

Herbert Mills, on the right, arriving at the Leenside Police Station in 1951 for the inquest on Mabel Tattershaw. Mills had approached the *News of the World* with his story of finding the body of a woman in the Orchard at Sherwood Vale. Full of conceit, and enjoying the limelight, he overreached himself with his tales and accurate knowledge of the crime and was subsequently arrested and charged with murder.

Mr Justice Byrne entering the Shire Hall in November 1951 to preside over the trial of Herbert Mills for murder. The nineteen-year-old Mills was found guilty and, showing no remorse, was hanged in Lincoln Prison on 11 December 1951.

A view towards the Castle and Brewhouse Yard from the waste land near Castle Road, 1950. This area of tightly packed houses was the last of the condemned properties of Broad Marsh to be demolished. St Nicholas' Church School, in the centre, built in 1859, had not been used as a school since 1912 and was to be pulled down in 1956 when the People's College of Further Education was built. Beyond the school building is the Trip to Jerusalem and the seventeenth-century buildings of Brewhouse Yard, now converted into a museum.

Jessamine Cottages in 1956 just prior to their demolition. These cottages, below the Castle in Workhouse Yard, were built in 1729 as a workhouse for the parish of St Nicholas. In 1815 the building was converted into cottages and was an attractive sight from the Castle walls. They were unappreciated until after they had been pulled down.

The gatehouse of Nottingham Castle from the Castle grounds in 1959. The gatehouse or barbican contains the last remains of the ancient castle but was rebuilt in 1908 when it unfortunately lost most of its character. The view towards the city was still unspoilt by multi-storey car parks and offices – the Council House dominating the skyline.

The Trip to Jerusalem in 1959, one of the most famous public houses in the country. Although the date, 1189, on the wall is no longer accepted as the year of its origin, there was an ale house on this site in the Middle Ages. This building dates from the early eighteenth century when it was known as The Pilgrim.

Adventurous children testing the ice on the Grantham Canal in 1953. The nearby swans watch cautiously from their small pool of water cleared of ice by the local residents.

An electrician with a considerable task – planning where to install his outsize loudspeakers for the best effect at an outdoor event, 1950s.

The stalls and balcony of the Scala Cinema in the 1950s. The building opened in 1875 as the Alexandra Skating Rink but, within a year, was converted into the Talbot Palace of Varieties. In 1901 the building had another change of use when it became a cinema, known as the King's Theatre, and was renamed the Scala in 1913. The cinema had several more changes of name before finally closing down in 1979.

A lively scene at the Goose Fair on the Forest in 1951. The time is late afternoon and families are enjoying the atmosphere and fun. Dominating this part of the fair is the latest riding machine, known as the Jets, but in the background are some of the traditional entertainments, such as the helter-skelter and the swing-boats.

Broad Marsh in 1959 still awaiting a permanent use. Fairs and exhibitions were staged here in the years after the Second World War but the City Council was still undecided as to its long-term future. As a short-term solution a bus station was sited here which remained until the Broad Marsh Shopping Centre was built. On the right is the High Pavement Unitarian Church and beneath it the viaduct of the Great Central Railway. The buildings in Broad Marsh on the left include the small factory in which John Player began his cigarette business.

Trivett Square in 1959: not strictly a square but the old thoroughfare leading to Short Stairs. This area has not changed greatly although most of the garment and lace manufacturers and wholesalers who occupied these buildings have closed down or moved away.

The workroom of the Castle Embroidery Company, Normanton Street, Broad Marsh, 1953. This was one of the many garment manufacturers in the city which made Nottingham, with Leicester, the centre of the making-up industry in this country.

Lower Parliament Street, 1950. This road was built through the slums of Sneinton in the early 1930s to link up with Canal Street. The building on the left was built by R. Cripps & Co. in the late 1930s as a garage but it was requisitioned by the National Fire Service at the beginning of the Second World War. Subsequently, Boots Pure Drug Co. Ltd acquired the building for offices but it has now been demolished to be replaced by the National Ice Centre. In the background is Pullman's, a well-known and popular drapery store.

The Old Market Square in 1950. The layout of the square was due for another change during the 1950s, with the removal of the statue of Queen Victoria to the Victoria Embankment Memorial Gardens. The roundabout which replaced the statue was the first of a succession of schemes for controlling the traffic in the square, all with varying degrees of success.

Sir Anthony Eden speaking to a large crowd of people in the Old Market Square in May 1955. Sir Anthony succeeded Sir Winston Churchill as Prime Minister in April of that year and immediately called a general election. The Conservatives won the election but, following the British withdrawal from Suez in 1956, Sir Anthony Eden resigned as Prime Minister on the grounds of ill-health.

Right: Winter sun casting shadows on the cobbles at the bottom of Market Street in 1959. Although not easy to walk on, these cobbles were more attractive than the bland road surfaces used now. Griffin's Corner, as this was known, was a rendezvous as well known as the lions in front of the Council House.

Below: The Victorian corner premises of Lister Gate and Castle Gate in 1956. Weavers Vaults and off-licence are on the left with, adjoining them, Dewhurst who owned a number of butcher's shops in the city. On the first floor is the Silver Mirror Photography Co. and below to the right are Lennon Bros, tobacconists, another Nottingham firm with several outlets.

Players Please
BRADLEY'S
ALES
WAY OUT
CITY
A1
KEEP
LEFT
NNU 233

The Victoria Railway Station in 1953, when travel to all parts of the country by rail was still possible. The station remained for another fourteen years before it was closed under the Beeching axe. The trolley-bus in the foreground is a Notts. & Derbys. Traction Co. vehicle on the Ripley to Nottingham service, one of the longest routes in the country. This was the year these trolley-buses ceased operation.

Passengers with a purposeful tread, crossing the bridge between platforms at the Victoria Railway Station in 1951. This station, designed by A.E. Lambert, who was also responsible for the Midland Railway Station, had great character, and its demolition in 1967 is still regretted.

An excursion to Crewe from Nottingham in 1955, organised by the local branch of the Railway Correspondence and Travel Society. This appears to be a wet day but it has not dampened the enthusiasm of these train-spotters searching for the best position to take their photographs.

The 1960s

Boys fishing in the Fairham Brook at Clifton in 1966. This simple pleasure of children playing in their school holidays is perhaps now only seen in rural areas.

The extension of Maid Marian Way to Chapel Bar in 1964. The Corporation's plans were for an inner ring road to continue up to Canning Circus and run through part of the General Cemetery to St Ann's and Sneinton. Fortunately, the scheme was never completed but the legacy of Maid Marian Way still remains.

Newdigate House, beyond the door of the old Manor House on Castle Gate in 1964. By good fortune, Newdigate House was saved when Maid Marian Way was built and it was restored in 1966. This is probably the most famous house in Nottingham, being the residence from 1705 to 1711 of Marshal Tallard, who was captured at the Battle of Blenheim. The Marshal was only nominally a prisoner, being allowed into the town and to visit local dignitaries.

Broad Marsh viewed from the Castle in 1968 at the beginning of the development of the Broad Marsh Shopping Centre. The shops on Carrington Street in the distance were due to be demolished – the greatest loss being the Electricity Board showrooms, previously The James Store. The waste land in the middle distance, used as a temporary car park, was cleared of houses, shops and small factories in the 1950s.

The junction of London Road and Canal Street in 1969. St Patrick's Church on the left had lost its congregation and was to be demolished in 1979. The Plumptre Almshouses in the centre, although now replaced by new almshouses on Canal Street, were not pulled down and the building is now being restored for use as offices.

The ABC Cinema, Chapel Bar, in 1966. This cinema was opened in 1939 as the Carlton at the peak of the cinema-going era, when film shows almost always comprised two feature films and a newsreel. Sixty years later it is now a multi-screen cinema, and there are plans to demolish the building and construct a multiplex cinema and hotel on the site.

An incident on Long Row West in 1966. Firemen are fighting a fire in the Cavendish furniture store, which damaged the upper floors and would give the shop another reason for a bargain sale. The Odeon Cinema on the left is advertising the last few weeks of the showing of 'The Sound of Music' and in the background, the Albert Hotel on Derby Road can be seen displaying its name on the roof.

A well-known scene until the late 1960s: Long Row West with the characteristic frontage of the Black Boy Hotel dominating the street, which was the poorer when the hotel was pulled down in 1969. For decades the hotel had been host to actors and actresses, politicians, businessmen, commercial travellers and Nottingham folk who would meet their friends in the American Bar or restaurant.

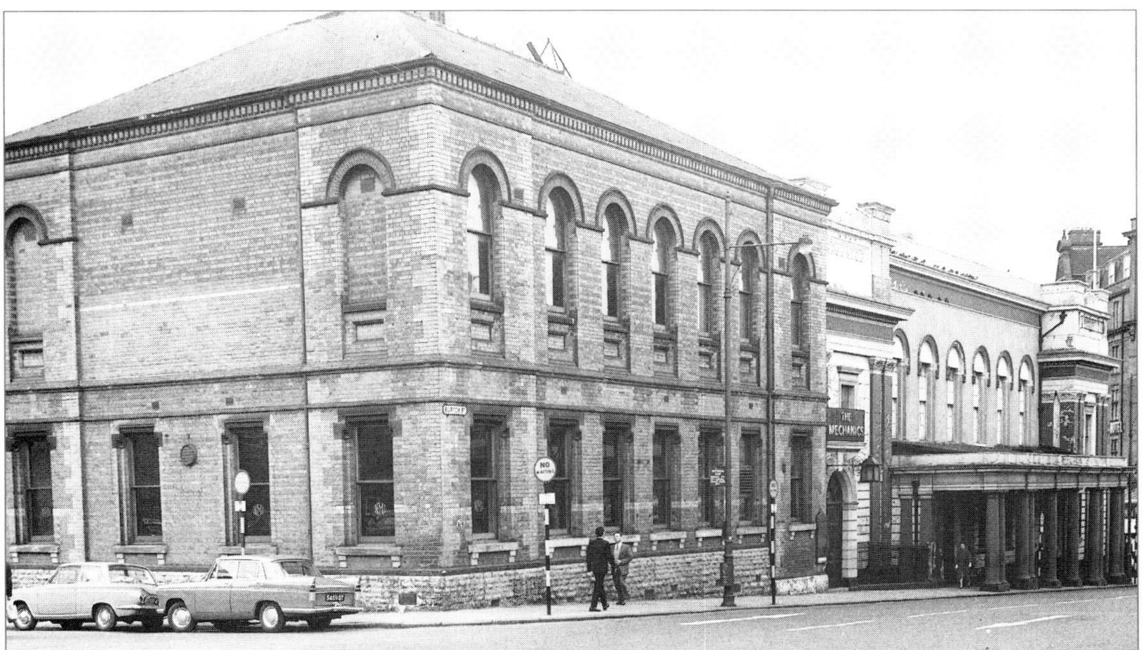

The Mechanics Institute and Hall on Burton Street in 1964, the year of their demolition. The Mechanics Hall on the right was built in 1869 after the original building was destroyed by fire. Many famous personalities visited the hall including Charles Dickens, Jenny Lind and Fanny Kemble before it was converted in 1916 to a cinema. Birkbeck House, named after the founder of the Mechanics Institute movement, was built on this site in 1965 and there are now plans for its rebuilding.

Two young girls enjoying a sedate swing in a local park in 1966. Nottingham is fortunate in having many parks and open spaces, particularly to the north and west of the city centre.

Sunbathers at Bulwell Lido in June 1966. This photograph was taken at a time when lidos were fashionable and Nottingham possessed three of them – the other two being Carrington and Highfields. Although apparently a hot day, there do not appear to be many swimmers in the pool.

Children frolicking at Highfields Lido in 1964. The lido was opened in 1924, the same year as the University Park was laid out, and quickly became popular. It closed in 1981.

Benita Myers on the left taking a photo for the family album at the Trent Boating Association Regatta at Colwick in 1966. Cyril Myers and his wife pose with daughter Jacki and friend – Lydia Frasier – on their boat *Cyrella*.

A tranquil scene at Trent Bridge in 1966 during the England versus West Indies Test Match. This was before many major changes at the ground – apart from the splendid electronic scoreboard which has now been replaced by a new scoreboard with a tall Notts. County Council office building behind it. The match resulted in a win for the West Indies by 139 runs.

An incident in the Nottingham Forest versus West Bromwich Albion match at the City Ground in September 1966. With the Albion goalkeeper beaten, Joe Baker prepares to shoot the ball into the unguarded net but a split-second later the referee blew his whistle for offside. The match resulted in a 2–1 win for Forest. This was to be Nottingham Forest's best season, since winning promotion to the First Division in 1957, finishing second to Manchester United.

Two teams of oarsmen in a race on the River Trent near the Suspension Bridge in 1965. With the opening of the National Water Sports Centre at Holme Pierrepont, Nottingham has become the Mecca for amateur and professional rowers.

A sunny Bank Holiday Monday on the Forest in 1960. These sportsmen are taking part in the Queen of the Midlands Bowls Tournament. Although an amateur game, it is being played with concentration and watched keenly by the spectators.

The headstock of Clifton Colliery just before the pit closed in 1969. The Nottinghamshire coalfield was mainly to the north and west of the city and this colliery was the most southerly until the opening of Cotgrave Colliery in 1964. Clifton Colliery was in production for almost a hundred years having been officially opened in 1870.

A familiar sight in the 1960s but now only a memory – a coalman delivering coal by the sack in Forest Fields.

A pair of Shipstone's greys pulling a dray loaded with barrels of beer near the Scotholme Hotel on Radford Road in 1968. The nearby Shipstone's Star Brewery was Nottingham's major brewery and their dray-horses were a frequent sight on the city's roads. These beautiful horses were retained by the brewery for publicity purposes for some years after they were essential. The brewery closed in 1994 and has now been converted into offices and apartments.

A snow-plough clearing snow from Mansfield Road, Daybrook, 1963. Fortunately, the Midlands do not often experience such bad weather as this. In the background are the offices of the Home Brewery Company which were designed by T. Cecil Howitt. Construction of the building began in 1939 but the tower was not completed until the early 1950s. Brewing ceased here in 1996 and this building is now being converted into offices for Nottinghamshire County Council.

Harry Worth on the left, joining in a publicity promotion for the Locarno Bingo Hall on St Ann's Well Road in 1964. This was originally the Victoria Ballroom but, when bingo became popular in the 1960s, this hall and many cinemas in the city were converted for the new pastime.

The launch of the *Bedside Playboy* at W.H. Smith & Son, Wilford Road in 1966. Twenty-one year old Bunny Girl, Dolly Read, is posing in a publicity shot with male admirers crowding around her.

The 1970s and 1980s

The Victoria Clock Tower in 1973, now only a folly, dwarfed by the Victoria Centre flats in the background. The young folk of Nottingham probably wonder at the reason for such an edifice and the older citizens know that the great railway station which adjoined it was needlessly destroyed in 1967.

A continental atmosphere on Angel Row in 1989. The Bell Inn has spread its tables and chairs onto the pavement and fortunately the weather is kind. This stretch of Angel Row possesses a number of interesting buildings including Bromley House, in the centre, built in 1752 and since 1821 the home of the Nottingham Subscription Library. The mock-Tudor building beyond was for many years the premises of Pearson & Pearson, a shop where mothers-to-be could buy their splendid coach-built perambulators.

Pearsons department store on Long Row West in 1987, the year before it closed down. This shop, which opened in 1889, was one of Nottingham's institutions and is sadly missed. During alterations to the property in the early 1990s, structures dating back to the eighteenth century were discovered behind the façade and the building was given Grade II listed status. (See page 113.)

Pearsons shop frontage in Upper Parliament Street in 1988. This building, named Empire House, was designed by T. Cecil Howitt for A.B. Gibson Ltd, wholesale provision merchants. In 1962 Pearsons bought the property and extended the 1933 façade. When Pearsons closed in 1988, this building was demolished.

Lambert's factory in 1988. This factory, with its distinctive clock tower, was built in 1863 by William and John Lambert for their lace dressing business. In 1979 the factory closed but was listed as a Grade II building. During renovations to the building in 1990, a high wind caused the tower to collapse and an identical clock tower was rebuilt to replace it.

The curtain-walls of the Victoria Centre flats dominating this view from the Newton Building of the Nottingham Trent University in 1988. Beyond and stretching to the skyline are the terraced houses of St Ann's.

A bird's-eye view of the Victoria Clock Tower showing the fine architecture surrounding the cupola, 1973. Whatever one's opinion of the Victoria Centre flats, they provide wonderful views over the city.

St James's Street in 1973 – one of the old thoroughfares of Nottingham. The street contains buildings in a variety of styles, with a number of Georgian houses and Victorian buildings intermingled with modern structures. The second building on the right was the Old Malt Cross Music Hall which opened in 1877. After a long period as a drapery warehouse and then an Italian restaurant, it has now been restored as a music hall with the original gallery preserved.

Lister Gate precinct in 1988. Once a busy road to and from the south of the city, it has now been pedestrianised and is a haven for shoppers, stallholders, buskers and itinerants. Nottingham's main shopping streets are similar to streets in other major cities, now lined with branches of national shops, with only the occasional old-established local business.

Schoolboys buying sweets from Edwin Malt's shop in Chandos Street, Netherfield in 1970. This type of general store which sold most items was then on the corner of many streets. The coming of supermarkets and shopping centres saw the demise of these shops which caused a great loss to the community.

Alan Trease examining a glass of wine preparatory to tasting it at Weavers, Castle Gate in 1978. The business was begun in 1844 by Edwin Weaver and purchased by George Trease in 1897 and has remained in the Trease family ever since. One of the splendid Georgian houses in Castle Gate is also owned by Weavers and used for wine-tastings and buffets, while the cellars and caves beneath are employed for storing their wine.

1988. Once described as 'the ugliest road in Europe', Maid Marian Way has not improved with age. None of the new buildings constructed along the road have any style and dwarf the few remaining historic houses on nearby Castle Gate. On the skyline to the left is the round tower of the Jubilee Wing of the old General

The Lace Centre on Castle Road in 1988. The reconstruction here of Severn's, a medieval building from Middle Pavement, was the compromise reached when it was threatened with demolition in 1968.

Right: Two notable landmarks of Nottingham rising above the roofs of the city in 1988. The tower of the Albert Hall on the left was built in 1907–9 by A.E. Lambert who also designed both the city's railway stations. For three-quarters of a century the Albert Hall was a Methodist Church and also Nottingham's main concert hall. The last service was held here in November 1985. St Barnabas' Cathedral, on the right, was designed by A.W. Pugin and built in 1841–4. Its construction caused considerable controversy, being described as 'the new Romish Meeting House on Derby Road'.

Below: The Nottingham Harmonic Society Choir and Orchestra conducted by Noel Cox in the familiar setting of the Albert Hall in 1972. The society was founded in 1856 and has established itself as one of the leading choruses in the country. Since its inception, many distinguished conductors have been associated with the choir, including Sir Arthur Sullivan, Sir Henry Wood, Sir Adrian Boult, Sir Malcolm Sargent and more recently Richard Hickox and Sir David Willcocks. Under their current Director of Music – Neil Page – the choir has given many fine performances at the Royal Concert Hall.

Bottle Lane in 1989, one of the oldest streets in Nottingham although none of the remaining buildings are ancient. In the Middle Ages this street led from the Norman borough to the English borough around St Mary's Church. When the Great Central Railway tunnel was being excavated beneath this street in the 1890s, many caves were discovered here and were subsequently filled in.

The old London Road Low Level Railway Station in 1987. It was built by T.C. Hine in 1857 for the Great Northern Railway Company. This station was mainly used for goods traffic following the construction of the Victoria Railway Station. Passenger trains stopped calling here in 1944 but goods trains continued to use the station until 1972. Since then various schemes have been proposed for the building and it is now being renovated for use as a leisure and fitness centre. The modern building in the background is the city's Eastcroft incinerator.

The Lace Market from Collin Street in 1987 with, in the foreground, the old Great Central Railway viaduct decorated with murals. The High Pavement Unitarian Chapel on the left was being renovated before being opened as the Lace Hall and has now been reincarnated as a Pitcher and Piano bar-restaurant. St Mary's Church on the right appears hemmed in by the Victorian offices and warehouses.

Green's Mill on Sneinton Hill in 1988. The mill was restored to full working order in memory of George Green, the mathematician, who spent most of his life here. Born in 1793, the son of the miller, he became famous for his mathematical theorems although these were not fully appreciated until after his death. The mill was gutted by fire in 1947 when it was being used as a shoe polish factory and remained derelict until 1974 when a fund for its restoration was set up.

A young girl clutching her mother's hand, fascinated by the reflections in the canal, *c.* 1988. This stretch of the Nottingham Canal has taken on a new image with riverside bars and restaurants replacing old warehouses.

A girl in a wetsuit in a predicament on Queens Drive in 1987. This is her twenty-first birthday – tied to the traffic-lights and apparently abandoned – although she seems to be in good spirits.

Modern Nottingham

St Mary's Church in 1996. The Mother Church of Nottingham has the appearance if not the status of a cathedral; it was mentioned in Domesday Book. The present building dates from the fifteenth century. The church was in danger of collapsing in the nineteenth century and was completely restored by Sir Gilbert Scott and William Moffatt.

The Nottingham Ice Stadium in 1997. The stadium was built in 1939 but it was not until after the end of the Second World War that the Nottingham Panthers ice hockey team was formed and began playing here. Those were exciting days and the top players of that era such as Chick Zamick, Les Strongman and Kenny Westman are still remembered. In recent years the Panthers have been re-formed and attract large crowds. The phenomenal success of the Nottingham ice-dancers Jayne Torvill and Christopher Dean has brought added interest to ice-skating and the National Ice Centre is now being built on this site.

Contrasting styles of architecture in George Street in 1992. On the immediate left is the fantastically decorated office of Watson Fothergill who designed many splendid houses and public buildings in the city. Beyond are two interwar buildings and the tower of the Central Methodist Mission, and in the background are the tower blocks of the Victoria Centre flats.

The Magistrates Courts on the bank of the Nottingham Canal in 1996. This modernistic building was opened in 1995 to house the courts which were previously held at the Guildhall. This part of Nottingham – once Midland Railway land – has now been transformed by new and renovated buildings.

Nottingham Castle from the Inland Revenue complex in 1996. Compared to the castle, the Inland Revenue buildings are ultra-modern but the design was modified to satisfy critics of the original plan. Viewed from the castle, the complex is bold and imaginative.

A view from ground level of the Council House in 1996. The controversial group of life-size figures in the foreground was sculpted by Richard Perry and was unveiled by Princess Anne in 1986. On the right is a children's roundabout, enlivening the Old Market Square.

Will this be his lucky day? A job-seeker in 1992 scanning the columns of advertisements in the *Nottingham Evening Post*.

A couple feeding a flock of pigeons in St Peter's Square in 1996. Pigeons in city centres have always been a problem and various deterrents have been tried without success – the latest suggestion is to introduce a hawk into Nottingham's city centre.

Drury Walk, one of the entrances to the Broad Marsh Shopping Centre in 1996. Most of the people using this entrance to the centre are unaware they are following in the footsteps of countless people entering or leaving the old town of Nottingham by Drury Hill. At the foot of the escalator through these doors, the city authorities have now re-opened the underground caves as a tourist attraction.

The Old Corner Pin at the junction of Clumber Street and Upper Parliament Street in 1996. Now only an imitation of the former building on the site, this is the Disney Store, which was succeeded by a fast-food outlet and is now a branch of Etams. The old building was a well-known public house dating from the eighteenth century, originally known as the George and later as the Horse and Groom, before becoming the Old Corner Pin in 1912.

Pearsons building in 1991, shored up after there was danger of the façade collapsing. When Pearsons closed in 1988, a development company began to renovate the property but this was halted until the façade was stabilised. The premises re-opened as two retail shops in 1994 but a major fire in 1996 entirely gutted the interior and all the restoration work had to be repeated. (See page 97.)

The Nottingham Evening Post building viewed from the Newton Building of the Nottingham Trent University in 1997. For a century the Guardian Office, as it was first called, had graced Sherwood Street and Forman Street but it has now been demolished to make way for a multiplex cinema. The newspaper is being produced in new purpose-built offices on Canal Street and printed in Derby.

Two favourite rides at the Goose Fair in 1996 – a giant wheel and the helter-skelter. The Ferris wheel on the left took several days to erect and gives a thrill and a bird's-eye view of the fair to everyone who rides it. The helter-skelter, although more sedate, gives excitement and an itchy feeling from the mats used on the slide.

A family enjoying the pleasures of the Goose Fair in 1996. Nottingham's ethnic communities are now well integrated in the city and take part in all Nottingham's activities.

Youngsters experiencing the thrill of a ride on the 'Dancer', one of the latest machines at the Goose Fair in 1996. Each year these imports from either the continent or America become more hair-raising.

The London Road High Level Railway Station in 1991. This station was built by the Great Northern Railway Company in 1897 but, following the construction of the Victoria Railway Station, it was mainly used for local passenger traffic. The bridge over London Road was demolished in 1978. In the background are Jesse Boot's first factories, which were pulled down in 1996.

John Lock on the left and Iain Smart surveying the demolition of Boots Island Street buildings in 1996. In 1923 the Prince of Wales was greeted by Boots employees standing outside the building on the left. (See page 36.) The new BBC Centre has now been built on this site.

The demolition of Boots Island Street warehouses in 1996. Jesse Boot began manufacturing drugs and toiletries here in the nineteenth century and gradually acquired the majority of the property in the district. These buildings were his first purpose-built factories and warehouses – completed in 1914. The site is now being redeveloped with modern offices replacing the old structures.

The 200-ton girder bridge spanning the Nottingham Canal being lowered to the ground before its demolition in 1996. This is one of the bridges which carried the Great Northern Railway and the London Road High Level Railway Station. A 1,000-ton Krupp's crane is lifting this great feat of engineering.

Two well-loved buildings with different stories to relate. The Theatre Royal on the left was built in 1865 by William and John Lambert to a design by C.J. Phipps. Frank Matcham made significant alterations to the theatre in 1897 and it continued to present plays, shows and pantomimes with all the great actors and actresses of the twentieth century. When the Theatre Royal was in danger of closure in the 1960s, the Corporation bought the theatre and refurbished it. The Nottingham Evening Post building on the right has, however, not survived. The building, from whose balcony election results were announced earlier in the twentieth century, was demolished in 1999 and is to be replaced by a multiplex cinema.

The beginning of a stage of the Kellogg's Cycle Race from the Old Market Square in 1994. This was also Festival Week in Nottingham, which added to the excitement. A group of police motor-cyclists are leading the racing cyclists, ensuring the route is kept clear.

The Council House dominating the scene from the Market Square House in March 1997. This is the occasion of the visit of Queen Elizabeth II to Nottingham to celebrate the centenary of the city. Queen Victoria honoured Nottingham by granting it city status in 1897 to coincide with her Diamond Jubilee. The Council House, now seventy years old, has become the best known feature of Nottingham.

Sneinton Market in 1993 with the locals choosing bargains from the stalls. The market has been a part of the Sneinton scene for over a hundred years and has been retained in the recent redevelopment of the area. The tower of the Victoria Leisure Centre in the background is another feature of the district – its future still undecided. The old Ragged School on the far left has fortunately been saved and is now the headquarters of the Nottinghamshire Wildlife Trust.

A serious business – choosing sweets from a confectionery stall at Sneinton Market in 1992. This is one of the most popular stalls in the market, selling a range of sweets and chocolates at bargain prices.

Acknowledgements and Picture Credits

I am most grateful to Mrs May Sentance and Miss Dorothy Stevenson, the daughters of Frank Stevenson, for again allowing me to have access to many of their father's fine photographs. I also wish to thank the following for the loan of photographs: G.H.F. Atkins, The Boots Company PLC, A. Corner, C. Hardy, J.W. Lock, J. Middleton, Nottingham City Council: Local Studies Library, *Nottingham Evening Post*, Nottingham Harmonic Society, D. Parker, W. Smalley, A. Trease.

I would also like to thank Joan Bray, Dorothy Ritchie and the staff of the Local Studies Library for all their kindness and help.

My special thanks are due to my wife Margaret for her continued help and encouragement.

Jayne Torvill and Christopher Dean in front of the Council House, early 1980s. This couple, the most famous ice-dance team in the world, have brought great prestige to their home city and have encouraged others by their example.